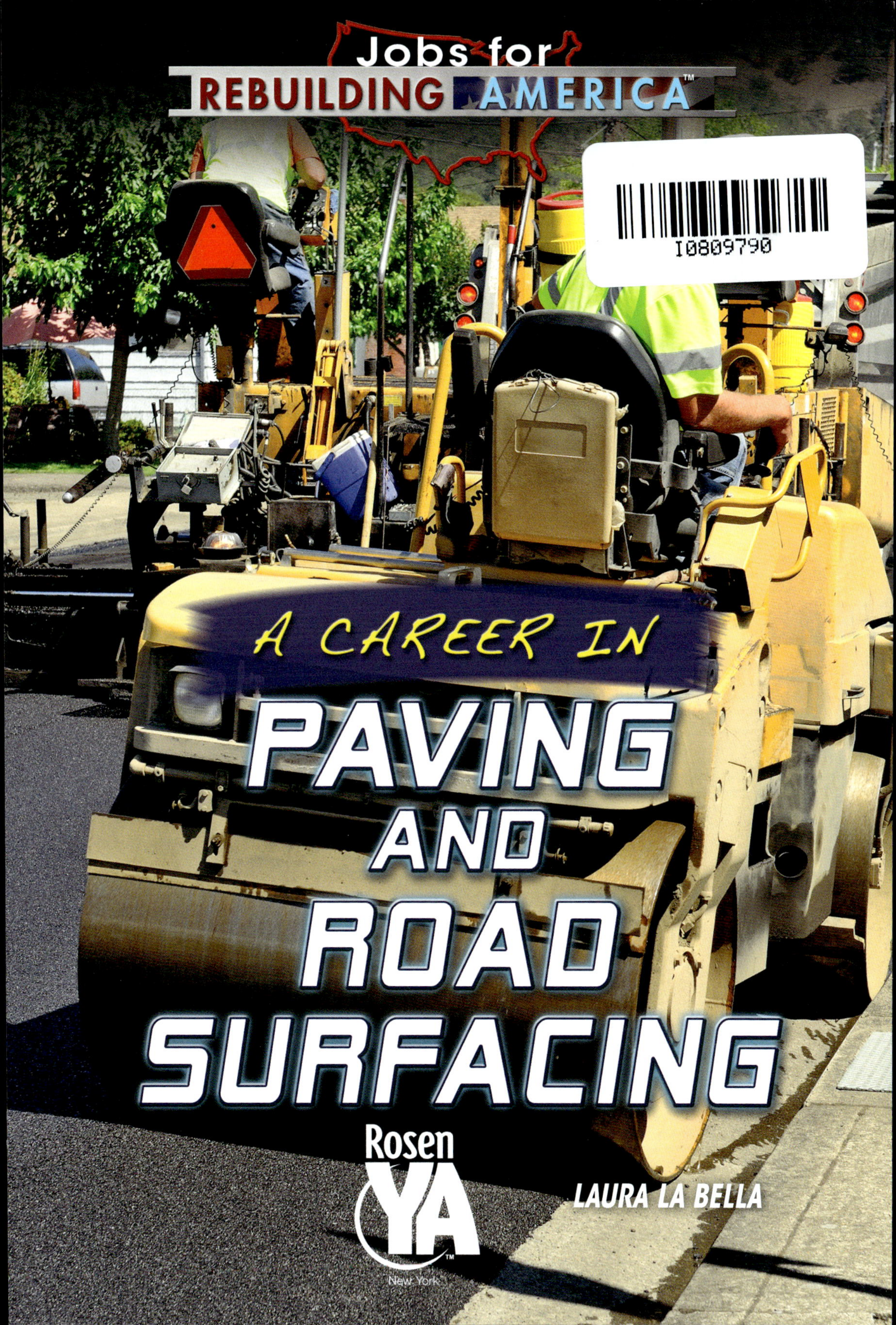

Jobs for REBUILDING AMERICA™

A CAREER IN PAVING AND ROAD SURFACING

Rosen YA™
New York

LAURA LA BELLA

Published in 2019 by The Rosen Publishing Group, Inc.
29 East 21st Street, New York, NY 10010

First Edition

Library of Congress Cataloging-in-Publication Data

Names: La Bella, Laura, author.
Title: A career in paving and road surfacing / Laura La Bella.
Description: New York : Rosen Publishing, 2019. | Series: Jobs for Rebuilding America | Audience: Grades 7–12. | Includes bibliographical references and index.
Identifiers: LCCN 2017058546| ISBN 9781508180029 (library bound) | ISBN 9781508180036 (pbk.)
Subjects: LCSH: Road construction workers—Vocational guidance—United States. | Road construction industry—Vocational guidance—United States. | Roads—United States—Design and construction.
Classification: LCC HD8039.R62 L3 2019 | DDC 625.7023/73—dc23
LC record available at https://lccn.loc.gov/2017058546

Manufactured in the United States of America

CONTENTS

INTRODUCTION

Every single day, the American public takes advantage of its nation's infrastructure. Every time someone visits a library, drives on city streets, travels on a highway, crosses a bridge, attends school, or stops at a railroad crossing, that person are utilizing our nation's infrastructure.

Infrastructure is a term that refers to the basic physical systems of our country—the built environment that is the marker of a modern, relatively efficient society. This built environment includes the roads, waterways, bridges, ports, subways, airports, and railways used for transportation. The energy and electrical systems, such as our national grid, used to power homes, businesses, and cities, is also part of our infrastructure. The public places and spaces, such as libraries, schools, municipal buildings, and parks and trails used for learning, public life, and health, are also part of it. So are the many systems that exist underground or are otherwise hidden, like public water resources and sewage systems, that enable our communities to have clean water and efficient wastewater management. All of these systems are part of an interconnected system that supports our everyday activities.

American infrastructure enables the economic activities that also dominate our lives. Jobs related to infrastructure account for nearly 11 percent of the nation's workforce.

Road paving and resurfacing crews are responsible for ensuring that millions of miles of highways, roads, and streets are smooth and drivable.

Many of these jobs offer competitive wages, require less formal schooling than white-collar work, and provide on-the-job training. Demand for such jobs is also expected to grow as the need increases to improve, replace, and modernize our current infrastructure.

There are a number of infrastructure sectors, including energy, telecommunications, public works, and water, and all of them offer immediate employment opportunities. Among the most crucial of the infrastructure systems—and one in which jobs are readily available—is transportation.

Across all fifty states, there are more than 4.09 million miles (6.6 million kilometers) of rural roads, city streets, highways, and expressways. These roadways are used each and every day to carry goods, haul freight, and transport people to and from work and school. Roadways are crucial to American life. They serve to connect the nation's cities, suburbs, and rural communities. They enable travel for work or recreation.

But American roadways are failing. According to a report from TRIP, a national transportation research group, only 28 percent of our nation's major roads are in good condition. The remaining 72 percent are rated as substandard or poor. Potholes, uneven road surfaces, congestion on roadways due to insufficient roads to handle increasing traffic, long commutes due to congested highways and crumbling bridges are all significant problems plaguing our nation's roadways. The state of our roadways is becoming an even bigger problem as travel continues to increase. In the last fifteen years, vehicle travel on American roads has increased by 15 percent. American commuters are suffering through long commutes due to increased congestion on the highways.

Improving our roadways is of immediate importance. Better roads can lead to safer travel and fewer accidents, more efficient traffic patterns that eliminate or lessen congested highways, and smoother roadways that make cargo and freight travel across the country faster and cheaper. Jobs in road paving and road surfacing will be in demand to help improve our deficient roadways. These jobs are essential to making sure America can run smoothly.

CHAPTER ONE

AMERICA'S ROADS AND HIGHWAYS

On August 1, 2007, the Interstate 35W bridge in Minneapolis, Minnesota, was carrying bumper-to-bumper traffic during the evening rush hour. Just after 6 p.m., the bridge suddenly collapsed into the Mississippi River. Thirteen people were killed and 145 were injured. In the days that followed the collapse, the public learned that the bridge had been classified as structurally deficient, which meant it was aging and in need of significant repairs. The bridge was also rated as "fracture critical," a designation that meant that if just one vital component of the bridge failed, the entire structure would collapse.

While it was later determined that the cause of the bridge collapse was a design flaw, not its structural integrity, the incident sparked an intensive look at the state of America's infrastructure. In the years since the Interstate 35W bridge collapse, America is still falling behind in its upkeep of its infrastructure. In 2017, the American Society of Civil Engineers (ASCE), which releases an annual infrastructure report card, gave our nation's infrastructure a grade of D+.

Damaged roadways, including those with potholes and uneven asphalt, can cost drivers plenty of money in vehicle repairs and can even prove dangerous or fatal.

The ASCE's report looks at a range of categories, including aviation, bridges, drinking water, energy, ports, railways, roads, schools, transit, and more and grades each on capacity, condition, funding, and public safety. Since 1998, grades have been falling due to delays in maintenance and reductions in state and federal funding that are needed to make many of the necessary upgrades and repairs.

HOUSTON CITY LAYOUT MAY HAVE WORSENED HURRICANE HARVEY FLOODING

American roadways, bridges, airports, and sewers are just one part of the country's infrastructure. City planning, or how a city was designed and built to accommodate growth, can impact traffic congestion, roadway travel, and storm water management. Houston, Texas, experienced firsthand the impact of poor city planning during Hurricane Harvey.

Hurricane Harvey made landfall on Friday, August 25, 2017, between the cities of Port Aransas and Port O'Connor, Texas, about 150 miles (241 km) south of Houston. The Category 4 storm had winds of 130 miles (209 km) per hour and dumped more than 50 inches (127 centimeters) of rain in and around Houston over a four-day period. While no city can plan for every natural disaster, especially one as unprecedented as Hurricane Harvey, some city planning experts agree that if Houston had planned out its city in a way that included more green land, it may have been able to lessen the impact of the storm's massive flooding.

Houston has seen a 23 percent increase in population since 2001. As a result, the city has undergone urban sprawl—that is, the development of urban space beyond the city borders itself. When this happens, cities need to accommodate the increase in population by adding new housing and apartment buildings, additional stores, more strip malls, extra paved streets, and extra parking lots. All of this added construction is accomplished with concrete, which doesn't absorb water like green space does. Parkland, trails, and green spaces around buildings all help absorb rainwater to help control flooding. The massive amount of concrete space may have made flooding by Hurricane Harvey much worse. According to an article on CNN, if a city balances its planning to include concrete building structures with ample amounts of green space, flooding, to a degree, can be controlled better.

PUBLIC WORKS

The nation's failing infrastructure now stands in great contrast to the massive public works projects that once served to modernize America in the 1930s and 1940s. Investing in infrastructure was one of the ways in which America's government and business leaders helped to develop a modern and economically stable nation. In an effort to lift America out of the Great Depression in the early 1930s as part of the New Deal set of policies, President Franklin D. Roosevelt helped fund infrastructure projects across the country to employ millions of people who lost jobs during the Depression and to modernize the nation.

According to the Roosevelt Institute, between 1935 and 1943 the federal government funded public works projects that included the construction of 572,000 miles (920,545 km) of rural roads, 67,000 miles (107,826 km) of city streets, 122,000 bridges, 1,000 tunnels, 1,050 airports and airfields, 4,000 airport buildings, 500 water treatment plants, 1,800 pumping stations, 19,700 miles (31,704 km) of water mains, 1,500 sewage treatment plants, 24,000 miles (38,624 km) of sewers and storm drains, 36,900 schools, 2,552 hospitals, 2,700 firehouses, and nearly 20,000 county, state, and local government buildings.

The New Deal provided much-needed employment for both skilled and unskilled workers while it enabled the United States to enter a modern age with infrastructure that could accommodate increases in vehicle, air, and rail travel, expanding imports and exports, and growing freight and cargo transport within our own nation.

A CENTER OF GAINFUL EMPLOYMENT

Infrastructure is the backbone of a healthy economy. When infrastructure is healthy and strong, it enables trade, helps businesses to grow, connects workers to their jobs, creates opportunities for struggling rural communities to link with

The Los Angeles freeways are a network of highways that serve more than 22 million people in the greater Los Angeles area. These are some of the thousands of major roads that keep Americans moving daily in their commutes and errands.

growing cities, and protects communities from unpredictable environmental disasters. Most importantly, a growing infrastructure creates jobs.

A review by the Brookings Institution of data from the US Bureau of Labor Statistics shows that fourteen million people work in jobs directly related to infrastructure. These jobs include railway engineers, electrical and telecommunication line installers, truck drivers, airline pilots, airline maintenance workers, construction workers, road pavers, delivery service drivers, transit workers, freight laborers, and more. These jobs are critical for a number of reasons: they provide good wages, require low formal education, have low barriers to entry, and are projected to grow over the next decade.

JOBS IN PAVING AND ROAD RESURFACING

Keeping our roadways smooth and passable is the job of a paving and road resurfacing crew. Like all forms of construction, new roads are needed as communities grow and spread out to new areas. Other times, roads become damaged or deteriorate and require repairs. A paving and road resurfacing crew is responsible for making sure new roads are constructed and existing ones maintained to ensure safety and ease of travel. Paving and resurfacing crews work on different types of roadway construction projects. Resurfacing a street addresses problems such as potholes, cracked pavement, bumps, or crumbling asphalt. Resurfacing is a less expensive, but short-term, solution to fixing a roadway.

Meanwhile, reconstructing a street is a more complex project. It can include fixing the street surface, constructing or reconstructing sidewalks and curbs, installing pedestrian ramps or bridges, improving safety by altering a street's curves or straightaways, adding traffic signals or street lights, changing the grading or slope to improve storm water runoff, or adding underground utilities. Street reconstruction involves extensive

Orange traffic cones and pylons, a common sight on roadways that are under construction, help to alert drivers to construction work, detours, or delays.

coordination between a local department of transportation and the community. It can include detours to reroute traffic and closed roads. It's also a lengthy project that can take three to five years from the design stages, which detail what the changes will be, to the construction stage, when physical work is being done on roadways.

OPPORTUNITY IN INFRASTRUCTURE

American infrastructure needs improvement, and many leaders have proposed spending to invest in many much-needed improvements to our roadways, waterways, and bridges, among other infrastructure needs. But who will do the work?

Nearly 40 percent of the workers currently employed in jobs related to infrastructure are nearing retirement. Even though infrastructure jobs pay well, there aren't enough younger workers ready to replace the aging employees who are moving into retirement. One reason for the downturn in workers is the lack of vocational training programs that are educating young people for jobs in fields such as construction, electrical work, and manufacturing. Those programs were pipelines for businesses in these sectors to attract skilled workers.

With more than 1 million miles (1.6 million km) of poor roads that require attention, along with those that may not be graded as poorly but still need repaving or maintenance, jobs in paving and road surfacing will be in demand. Jobs in paving and road resurfacing are available for those with both formal education, such as degrees in civil engineering, construction management, or architecture, as well as those with informal education or vocational training.

These jobs—such as paving crew laborer, paving- and surface-equipment operator, asphalt-paving foreman or supervisor, and paving superintendent—are all open to workers with a high school education and a willingness to learn skills on the job. Employers are looking for job candidates who have the following skills:

- **Organization:** Employers are looking for job candidates who can handle a long-term project that requires attention to detail, diligent planning, and the management of a lot of different tasks.
- **Problem-Solving:** Some jobs will require candidates to think outside the box, brainstorm new ideas, and find solutions to problems as they arise.
- **Teamwork:** Infrastructure jobs are team based. You'll work with other people on projects where collaboration, communication, and teamwork as essential to success.
- **Attention to Detail:** Infrastructure jobs require attention to detail to ensure safety standards are met and plans are fulfilled according to the engineer or architects' schematics.
- **Technical Expertise:** Some math and science knowledge will be necessary, as will a willingness to learn about the construction field.
- **Physical Stamina:** Construction jobs, especially those that require physical work, require workers to lift heavy materials, operate large equipment, and be outside working in a range of weather conditions for long stretches of time.

CHAPTER TWO

PAVING CREW LABORER

Road paving and resurfacing crews are made up of several types of positions, each with individual and team-based responsibilities that assist the crew as a whole in accomplishing a road construction project. Among the jobs that make up the team are a paving crew laborer, paving- and surface-equipment operator, asphalt-paving foreman or supervisor, and paving superintendent.

While the paving crew laborer is the most entry-level position of all paving crew members, it is a position that is among the most crucial to the team. A paving crew cannot work efficiently or productively without at least one paving crew laborer on each project. The job is also a stepping-stone to more advanced paving crew positions that offer more responsibility, better pay, higher levels of skill, and opportunities for leadership.

WHAT DOES A PAVING CREW LABORER DO?

A paving crew laborer's main responsibility is shoveling and raking road-surfacing materials into an even, smooth surface.

A paving crew laborer can perform a wide range of jobs, from spreading asphalt and assisting the foreman to directing traffic around a work site.

These laborers may use a range of road-surfacing materials, which can include asphalt, concrete, composite pavement, gravel surfaces, and sealants. The position is also crucial because such laborers also assist others on the paving crew with their specific tasks. This allows them to get a glimpse of many different jobs and duties, and prepares them for advancement up the career ladder.

A paving crew laborer reports to the crew foreman. In addition to raking and shoveling roadway materials, the laborer also helps maintain paving equipment and cleans tools. Paving laborers need to communicate well with the other crew members as they work on a roadway. This ensures that crew members are clear about which portion of the project they are working on each day. Crew members also need to understand the daily goals the paving crew foreman has set, and all crew members must comply with the safety policies set for their particular job site.

Meeting their responsibilities helps laborers lay the groundwork for promotions to better positions on the paving crew. As their job duties and competence grow, laborers are promoted and given incremental salary raises. A paving laborer must be aware of his or her productivity. He or she must be efficient and detail oriented. Laborers often work on smaller aspects of a paving project or on parts of a job that prepare a portion of the project for other workers. If a laborer is slow or doesn't complete his or her work on schedule, it can hold up other crew members and affect the timely completion of a project.

HIGHWAY TRUST FUND HITS A POTHOLE

The federal government operates the Highway Trust Fund, a major source of funding for public roads, highways, bridges, tunnels, and public transit. The fund collects its money through the federal gas tax. By charging a tax of 18.4 cents per gallon of gasoline and 24.4 cents per gallon of diesel, the gas tax generates roughly $34 billion each year that is available to the fund to support repairs and improvements to the country's transportation system. The federal government currently spends about $50 billion a year on transportation infrastructure repair and improvements. The fund was scheduled to run out of money in 2016, but Congress stepped in and approved a bill that added money to the fund.

A bigger issue for the fund is the growing interest in electric cars. Electric cars are battery operated and require little or no gas. While they are a better choice for the environment, gas sales are impacted. As electric cars become more popular and more affordable, fewer people will be purchasing gas, which means even less money will be paid in gas tax, resulting in a smaller budget for the Highway Trust Fund.

SKILLS AND PHYSICAL REQUIREMENTS

Working as a paving crew laborer is physically demanding. In addition to shoveling, raking, and heavy lifting, laborers may be required to operate a jackhammer and other power tools and equipment. They help direct heavy equipment operators, and they perform grading checks to ensure the slope or incline of a road is correct.

Laborers work outside in hot and humid weather conditions, sometimes even in temperatures of 100 degrees Fahrenheit (37.7 degrees Celsius) or higher. For hours at a time, laborers continually shovel hot asphalt onto roadways and rake it to a smooth finish. Asphalt is a heavy paving material and shovelfuls can weigh 50 to 70 pounds (22.7 to 31.7 kilograms) each. The job also requires long periods of standing and waiting while other crew members complete their work. Laborers must be able to kneel, reach, climb, and balance. They should also have good eyesight and good peripheral vision since work could be happening all around them, not just in front of where they are standing.

Laborers often learn to operate various types of equipment, such as a skid steer, a pavement saw, and a jackhammer. A wide range of equipment knowledge is vital to moving up in position on a paving crew. The more skills a laborer acquires, the more versatile and skilled the laborer becomes. This means the laborer can earn a better salary and increase his or her value to the foreman or construction company he or she works for.

Paving crew laborers have highly physical jobs. They need to be strong, physically fit, and agile. Endurance and stamina are required for often long workdays. Some projects might involve six- or even seven-day work weeks.

Hours can be long, sometimes ten to twelve hours a day. Depending on the location of the roadwork and the scope of the job, some paving crews work in the evenings and on weekends. In the northeastern part of the country, in states such as New York, Maine, Massachusetts, and Pennsylvania, all of which experience heavy snowfall and cold temperatures for six months of the year, roadwork projects can be completed only during the spring and summer months. In these states, road paving and resurfacing projects often demand longer hours to account for the limited time frame in which a project must be completed.

In addition to physical skills, laborers must be team players and work well with others. A paving crew can include dozens of members; the size depends on the project. Communication skills, good reading and writing skills, and excellent listening are crucial for success. Laborers also must be safety conscious. Many road-paving crews work while traffic continues to pass alongside their work site. While traffic may be redirected around the work zone, moving vehicles present hazards to laborers and crew members. Road crew workers also have to make sure they keep an eye out for pedestrians as well as cars, for both their own safety and that of others.

STARTING AT THE BOTTOM

A position as a paving crew laborer requires no formal education beyond a high school diploma. There are also no requirements for professional certifications or licenses.

INTERESTING FACTS ABOUT ASPHALT

Asphalt, a road-paving material that consists of cement mixed with stone, sand, or gravel, covers more than 94 percent of our nation's roadways. Did you know the following facts about asphalt?

- In ancient Rome, builders used asphalt to help waterproof their aqueducts and reservoirs.
- The first asphalt street in the United States dates back to 1870.
- Asphalt is 100 percent recyclable, and it is reused on our roadways.
- Asphalt does not dissolve in water so it cannot contaminate streams or other bodies of water.
- Due to its strength under heavy weight and its ability to withstand a high volume of traffic, asphalt is the most popular material used to pave airport runways.

Paving crew laborers gain their skills on the job, with guidance from coworkers and superiors. As a result, there are no required internship or apprentice programs available to those who are looking for more experience. However, apprenticeship

Paving crew laborers can gain experience on the job and work their way up to positions of more responsibility and better pay, including eventually getting on a management career track.

programs exist for those who would like to pair their on-the-job training with classroom instruction.

Classroom instruction might include learning in subject areas such as signaling, blueprint reading, understanding and using proper tools and equipment, and the importance of following health and safety policies and procedures. Apprenticeship programs often pair this classroom learning with specialized training in an area such as building construction, demolition and deconstruction, environmental safety and remediation, road and utility construction, tunneling, masonry and bricklaying, landscaping, and pipeline construction.

Job opportunities in building and maintaining roads will remain steady in the United States, as long as cars, trucks, and other vehicles require decent roads to drive on.

An apprenticeship can help position a paving crew laborer for career growth. The combination of on-the-job training and specialized instruction in a particular area of construction can prepare a laborer for immediate success in an entry-level position and for growth on the paving team.

A PROMISING OUTLOOK

According to the US Bureau of Labor Statistics, employment opportunities for all construction laborers, including paving and road-resurfacing laborers, are expected to increase by 13 percent from 2016 to 2026. This is a higher average than for construction occupations generally. Because laborers work in all fields of construction, including road paving and resurfacing, demand will be dependent on the overall increase in construction projects and funding for transportation infrastructure repairs and improvements.

CHAPTER THREE

PAVING- AND SURFACE-EQUIPMENT OPERATORS

Milling machines, asphalt pavers, compactors, graders, and skid steer loaders are the heavy-duty machines used by road-paving and resurfacing operators to construct, improve, or repair our nation's roadways, highways, city streets, and more. Paving and surface-equipment operators learn to drive, maneuver, or control these machines to get the job done.

WHAT DO PAVING- AND SURFACE-EQUIPMENT OPERATORS DO?

Paving- and surfacing-equipment operators control heavy-duty construction machines that are used to perform a variety of large-scale functions, such as delivering road-paving materials to a job site, removing damaged road surfacing, preparing roadways for resurfacing, spreading and leveling asphalt or other road-surfacing materials, smoothing asphalt and concrete, and grading a roadway to construction-design specifications.

One of the pieces of equipment used by pavers and road-resurfacing operators is a cold milling machine, which removes the top layer of a road's surface.

In order to operate these machines, paving- and surfacing-equipment operators must be knowledgeable about the individual functions of each machine, when each machine is used in the paving and resurfacing process, as well as how to maintain and repair them. They must be thoroughly trained in their use, with safety the foremost concern.

To operate these machines, they turn valves to regulate the temperature and flow of asphalt that is poured onto a roadbed. They ensure a constant flow of asphalt into a hopper, or holding container, that helps regulate an even distribution of paving material. Workers steer and guide machines to smooth the road surface and to compress it evenly. They also oversee the grading or slope of a road, and they monitor to make sure there is an even application of top-layer surfacing materials for a final finish.

Paving-machine operators must be knowledgeable about how each machine works and how the different controls and hand turns operate attachments that spread, vibrate, and level road-surfacing materials. They must monitor the application of surfacing materials to ensure that there is a smooth, even layer.

HEAVY WORK

A range of specialized heavy-duty machines are used on road-paving and resurfacing jobs. These machines improve efficiency on the job, increase productivity, and help the paving crew meet construction specifications for surface thickness and incline or decline in the grade of a roadway. Some of these include:

- **Milling machines.** Also called a cold planing machine, a milling machine is driven over a road surface. A large rotating drum scrapes a road surface to remove existing surface material. The milling machine grinds the removed surface material for later use. This recycling of surface material helps lessen the environmental impact of resurfacing a roadway. Depending on the job, a milling machine can remove just the top layer of paving material, or it can perform a full-depth removal of surface material down to the soil.

- **Skid steer loaders.** When road surfaces are fragile or damaged, sometimes a milling machine can create further harm to a road surface. A skid steer loader is then used instead. These small machines, which can pivot in tight spaces, are capable of ripping up soft or fragile road surfaces without inflicting further damage.
- **Asphalt pavers.** An asphalt paver is used to lay asphalt on the surface of a roadway. Surface material is placed in the machine's hopper, or container. An auger pushes the material onto the surface of a road. A screed levels the paving material on the roadway, resulting in a smooth, uniform surface.
- **Compactors.** A compactor is a machine that has a large, smooth drum attached to the front. It is used to compress surfacing material onto a roadway. The compactor follows the asphalt paver. Once the paver lays a smooth surface of material, the compactor's drum is driven over the material, pressing it onto the road surface.
- **Motor graders.** Grading a roadway surface ensures that the roadway has a specific slope. A slope ensures that rainwater runs off a roadway instead of collecting on its surface and creating puddles. Puddles of water on roadways are a driving hazard and can lead to accidents. A motor grader is used to make sure the desired slope designated for the project is accurate.

Another piece of equipment workers will encounter on a road crew is the motor grader. This machine spreads dirt or other surfacing materials and smooths it to an even finish.

SKILLS AND PHYSICAL REQUIREMENTS

Like paving and road-resurfacing laborers, most paving-machine operators learn the skills they need while they are on the job. It is a physically demanding position. In addition to sitting for long hours on a heavy-duty machine, paving-equipment operators may also need to shovel, rake, or lift heavy materials.

Important qualities and physical abilities for paving-machine operators include hand-eye coordination, agility, and mechanical aptitude. Equipment operators often operate machines that require the coordinated use of an operator's hands and feet to steer or operate the equipment. Operators should have steady control over their hands and feet so they can operate machinery precisely and in small, compact spaces. In addition, mechanical skills are helpful since operators often perform basic maintenance on the machines they use.

As with all outdoor construction gigs, paving-machine operators work in all kinds of weather conditions, particularly hot and humid ones. They also work in very little shade, with heat radiating off of the roadway surface. Workers can often get greasy, dirty, muddy, or dusty. Since they work alongside equipment that generates heat (and often on hot days), they are pretty much guaranteed to get sweaty as well.

Altogether, work on a paving crew consists of a variety of positions that all aid in constructing and repairing road surfaces. As a result, good communication skills are necessary to communicate concerns, understand the day's goals, and to convey problems and concerns while at work. Solid listening skills and an adherence to safety policies and procedures are crucial for success on the job.

Some equipment operators may work in remote locations away from family and friends or on large construction projects that could take weeks or months to complete.

THE INTERNATIONAL UNION OF OPERATING ENGINEERS

The International Union of Operating Engineers (IUOE) is a construction labor union that represents more than 15 million construction and infrastructure workers in the United States and more than 4.5 million workers in Canada. The union protects workers' jobs, establishes basic work terms and work conditions, sets the standards for educational levels and skill levels for workers, ensures equal compensation, and works to enforce safety policies and procedures. The union also negotiates benefits, such as affordable health care, for its members. The union offers training programs, apprenticeships, and certifications for heavy equipment operators, operating engineers, and pipeline workers. Many workers throughout North America who work in paving and road surfacing belong to the IUOE.

HOW TO QUALIFY

Many paving-equipment operators learn to operate a variety of machines while they are on the job. No formal education is required, but a high school diploma or its equivalent is necessary. Machine operators may also learn how to use paving and road equipment through an apprenticeship or by attending a vocational program.

For first-time machine operators, many will learn to use smaller equipment first before moving on to heavy-duty construction machinery. As they gain experience, paving-equipment operators will learn how to operate and maintain heavier equipment, such as skid steer loaders, milling machines,

An asphalt paving machine lays asphalt or other surfacing materials on roadways, bridges, parking lots, and city streets.

or bulldozers. These machines require more training and a foundation of knowledge of electronics.

For operators who choose to complete an apprenticeship, workers will learn how to operate heavy machinery in a three-to-four-year apprenticeship program. The apprenticeship program requires at least 144 hours of technical instruction and 2,000 hours of paid on-the-job training for each year of its duration. They will combine on-the-job training with classroom instruction that covers topics such as construction technology, safety practices, basic first aid, and reading construction plans and blueprints.

A final step in the process of road surfacing is accomplished using the roller, which presses the asphalt down and provides a smooth finish to the roadway.

Several organizations and contractor associations, such as the Heavy Construction Academy, International Union of Operating Engineers, Local 49 Training Center, and local community colleges, sponsor apprenticeship programs. The basic qualifications for applying to a program include a high school diploma, a minimum age of eighteen, a valid driver's license, and the ability to perform physical work. Because apprentices learn to operate a wider variety of machines than other beginning operators, apprentices often have better job opportunities and greater chances for career growth.

According to the US Bureau of Labor Statistics, the employment for construction equipment operators is projected to grow 12 percent by the year 2026. This increase will be faster than the average for all occupations, and the growth will occur across the entire construction industry. As spending on our national and local transportation infrastructure increases, jobs for paving-equipment operators will increase in response to the need to hire equipment operators to be members of paving and resurfacing crews.

CHAPTER FOUR

ASPHALT-PAVING FOREMAN

An asphalt-paving foreman supervises and coordinates the paving and resurfacing activities of the paving crew. The foreman is responsible for his or her crew and the work they perform spreading, rolling, tamping, and patching asphalt or other roadway materials on roadways, highways, city streets, parking lots, and other locations where road surfacing is needed.

WHAT DOES AN ASPHALT-PAVING FOREMAN DO?

An asphalt-paving foreman supervises and coordinates the various activities of the paving and resurfacing crew. He or she coordinates and oversees the training of new crew members, tours job sites to report on the progress of the crews to determine if they are staying on schedule, measures slope and material thickness to make sure crews are following the project's plans, and evaluates the work performance of his or her crews. In addition, the foreman supervises and coordinates his or her crews' assignments and activities, studies production schedules

A paving foreman has to keep the big picture in mind during a project, while also checking up on the work completed by his or her underlings, especially newcomers to the project and younger, more inexperienced laborers.

to make sure the crew meets important deadlines, and estimates when the job will be completed.

Foremen also set the crew's schedules, record and report work hours for the team, and collect paperwork from vendors that provide materials to the job site. A foreman is responsible for making sure invoices are delivered back to the construction company so suppliers can be paid for their supplies.

Foremen are also the public face of a job while onsite. They work with local governments to make sure the public knows when roads will be closed down or detoured to accommodate work crews. They make sure that the crew follows safety procedures to ensure a safe work environment for its members as well as the public, who may work near or pass by a work site during their commute.

WHAT IT TAKES TO BE A FOREMAN

An asphalt-paving foreman must have three to five years of experience working in the various jobs that make up a paving and resurfacing crew or an equivalent combination of education and training. He or she must be able to understand and know how to use all of the equipment on the project and be able to teach other crew members how to operate the machinery safely and efficiently.

Foremen must also be able to read project drawings and comprehend the instructions in memos and correspondence from the construction company. This job also requires at least an intermediate grasp of math, such as addition, subtraction, multiplication, and division in all units of measurement. He or she must be able to understand common fractions and be able to compute rates, ratios, and percentages. Some foremen need to be able to draw and interpret bar graphs as well.

Basic office skills are also required, such as the ability to type and use a computer. Knowledge of database software can also be helpful. A foreman must also possess good interpersonal and communication skills, as well as leadership and supervisory skills. These are essential because the majority of his or her time will be spent overseeing and managing work crews.

Foremen stay in constant contact with project managers and other off-site personnel. One of their responsibilities is to provide continual updates on the status of the roadwork being completed.

PHYSICAL REQUIREMENTS FOR A FOREMAN

As with all construction positions, a foreman will have to put in days of physical exertion. This will include standing for long periods of time; walking around a work site to assess progress or to determine problems; bending, crouching, and lifting; and carrying heavy materials. An eight-hour day is common, but so are ten-hour days. Many job sites have uneven terrain, and a foreman should be able to balance and navigate bumpy and jagged ground.

A candidate for this position should be strong and demonstrate dexterity. He or she may need to help the crew with carrying generators, construction materials, and various kinds of power and hand tools. He or she must also be alert at all times on a job site and know what the crew, as well as other crews on the project, are doing. Multiple work crews usually perform tasks at the same time, often on different aspects of a job. It's essential that the foremen of all the crews communicate with one another. Hazardous machinery requires that stringent safety measures be taken. Crews need to coordinate their jobs so that using equipment in one place doesn't endanger others or sabotage their work.

TRAINING A CREW

An asphalt paving and resurfacing crew foreman is responsible for more than just managing his or her crew. He or she must also be able to train his or her crew members to meet the demand for efficient, skilled crew members. To train crews effectively, foremen need to teach their crew members how to use the tools of the job, to understand the big picture of the job and how it fits into the scope of the larger project, and the importance of efficiency.

Foremen will begin training their paving crews by teaching them how to use hand tools, such as shovels, rakes, lutes, and hand tampers. Crew members will be taught how to use these

FOREMEN AND LEADERSHIP

A foreman has many roles: as a leader, teacher, a worker, and a motivator. Each day, as a crew gathers for work in the morning, the foreman needs to gather his or her team to share important information on the day's activities, remind workers of safety measures, and help kick off the day. A good one will convey a team-based message that helps set the tone for the workday, one that outlines clearly the foreman's expectations of the crew and what they should aim to accomplish by lunchtime, and by end of day.

Many foremen pull their teams aside numerous times a day. The foreman shares timely changes he or she receives from the project manager. Foremen will look to their team members for ideas, differences of opinion, or feedback on the project. This is also a time for the foreman to communicate directly with his or her team, and for the workers to share concerns or to work out issues and problems on the job.

tools correctly. Hand tools are essential before workers tackle the larger-scale machinery used on a job site.

It is also vital for foremen to teach crew members that their smaller project is part of a much larger construction job.

The foreman is usually the most experienced member of a paving crew. He or she has held nearly all of the jobs on the crew and has the experience to lead and train team members.

This helps workers understand that their work plays a bigger role in the success of a project that potentially impact the lives of thousands, or even millions, of people (namely, the people driving over the road they are working on).

Young crew members also get a taste of the business side of construction from their superiors. There is more to a construction project than just the small portion a crew member might be working on. A larger project has many sets of blueprints that all coordinate together to create a master plan. When a large-scale road project is approved, suppliers are asked to provide estimates for the costs of materials, managers are asked to estimate the number of workers they might need to complete the project, and crews must be assembled with a variety of workers and skill levels.

As entry-level crew members become more knowledgeable about the construction process, they become more aware of employment opportunities and can work with their foreman to create a career path to gain the skills they need to gain promotions to positions of greater skills and salary.

Construction projects are about getting the job done on time and on budget. Efficiency needs to be something crew members at all levels strive for, with guidance from foremen. Efficient crew members can be given an assignment and left unsupervised to complete it. Showing initiative also gets crew members noticed. When a portion of the job needs to be done, such as shoveling or raking, a laborer should take it upon himself or herself to complete this task without being asked. Such initiative is usually noticed and rewarded with greater responsibilities, promotions, and raises, even if that may take some time.

HIGHER UP THE LADDER

The foreman job is not an entry-level position. This job requires a high school diploma or a general education degree (GED) and three to five years of previous experience as a paving-equipment operator and as an asphalt-paving laborer. They must be able

As a foreman, much of one's workday may not be physical labor or operating equipment, but keeping track of progress and keeping the project on track by being in constant communication with various parties.

to operate the various kinds of paving machinery used on job sites, including a paver, roller, skid steer loader, backhoe, and milling machine.

Normally, foremen have a combination of experience and sometimes an apprenticeship experience before rising to the position of foreman. In an apprenticeship, a paving crew member will learn the various roles of the different crew members, and the apprentice will learn how to operate a wide range of equipment. He or she may also combine this on-the-job training with classroom learning that could include topics related to management and leadership, such as understanding how to read blueprints and construction documents, learning intermediate levels of math, and acquiring the skills needed to be an effective paving-crew manager.

CHAPTER FIVE

PAVING MANAGER OR SUPERINTENDENT

An asphalt-paving manager or superintendent is responsible for scheduling construction work. He or she coordinates multiple construction crews and plans and schedules a variety of necessary resources, such as equipment, subcontractors, and material suppliers. Ultimately, a paving manager is responsible for the completion of construction projects that are on time and on budget.

MANAGER OR SUPERINTENDENT DUTIES

An asphalt-paving manager or superintendent is a type of construction manager. He or she might also be called a general contractor or project manager. These people work on all types of construction jobs, from road paving and resurfacing projects to building bridges and erecting new schools and other types of public and private buildings. It is a versatile job that can require a manager to apply his or her skills in one area, such as road paving and resurfacing, to other types of related construction projects.

Paving superintendents and managers may have several work sites to oversee and often visit one or more of them in the course of a workday.

A construction manager is directly responsibility for all of the personnel, equipment, scheduling, safety, costs, and workmanship of a construction job. He or she also coordinates and manages any and all subcontractors hired for a project, as well as the safety of all workers on the job site. A paving manager often works for a large construction company or for a state or local department of transportation.

WHAT IT TAKES

As a paving manager, also referred to as a construction manager, one's duties include overseeing current employees as well as hiring new personnel. The manager must orient new workers to the job and make sure they understand the work and its requirements. Managers perform evaluations of workers and their performance on the job, and they sign off on all of the daily and weekly time logs.

Managers also supervise and direct the activities of project subcontractors, who might be hired to complete certain aspects of a construction project. Managers must evaluate their work to make sure they are following all safety policies and procedures and that their work is of high quality.

As the manager of multiple projects, managers also must pay attention to budgets and control costs on a job site. They need to make sure the paving foreman and their crews are using and maintaining machinery and equipment correctly.

Managers also need to continually evaluate the status of their projects and know where each project is when it comes to costs, schedules, job assignments, equipment needs, and any requirements of their crews on site, such as training, safety, or security needs. They are in charge of reporting on-site problems and communicating changes in the scope of a project to the crew foreman and any other project managers or directors. Because their work includes hiring and recruitment of workers, a manager must be knowledgeable of labor law, employment regulations, and company or department policies and procedures.

Construction managers must be as comfortable with standard business and project management software and paperwork as they are with heavy equipment operation or employee management.

Construction managers often have an office located at their construction company office or headquarters or at a government building if they work for a town, city, county, or state department of transportation. Their office will often have a desk, phone, computer, and other office resources and supplies. While they may do some work in their offices, managers work predominantly in the field, where they spend most of their time monitoring the status of ongoing jobs. When managers are in the field, they can assess problems, make decisions about construction activity, or deal with critical issues as they happen.

THE US DEPARTMENT OF TRANSPORTATION

The US Department of Transportation (USDOT) is a crucial agency of the US government. According to their website, the department's mission is to "serve the United States by ensuring a fast, safe, efficient, accessible and convenient transportation system that meets our vital national interests and enhances the quality of life of the American people, today and into the future."

The USDOT includes a number of offices that make safe travel a priority. These offices oversee all forms of transportation in the country, including highways, air travel, railways, and waterways, and include the National Highway Traffic Safety Administration, the Federal Aviation Administration, the Federal Highway Administration, the Federal Transit Administration, and the Maritime Administration.

The Transportation Department is overseen by the secretary of transportation, a cabinet-level position appointed by the president of the United States. The department was established by the US Congress in 1966.

A WORLD OF EXPERIENCE

The role of a paving manager or superintendent is a well-compensated and high-level one. Managers need to have a minimum of five years of experience as an asphalt-paving foreman on a highway or roadway construction project. Often times, experience working for a state or local department of transportation is preferred.

Key qualifications that employers look for in a paving manager are an ability to manage, supervise, schedule, and delegate on large projects. A manager must be a good decision maker. Managers work in environments where production and results are important. They must meet deadlines and stay under budget. Managers need to be knowledgeable of the various types of equipment used on the job, as well as any needs for additional resources a crew may have. They also need excellent communication skills.

Project management can also be a high-stress job. Managers are required to respond quickly to problems, assess situations as they change, and work efficiently under pressure to meet deadlines.

According to the US Bureau of Labor Statistics, there are numerous ways to enter the paving or construction management profession. Many construction and paving managers have a mix of formal education and work experience. It's important that managers have experience working on a paving crew so they can apply that first-hand knowledge while in a position of leadership. This combination of formal education and experience is particularly helpful for managers who are looking to be promoted to more advanced positions that include higher levels of leadership.

CLIMBING THE LADDER

Many paving-crew and construction project managers entered the profession with a high school diploma and worked their way up. They began as paving-crew laborers, moved into positions as paving-equipment operators, gained experience as a paving-crew foreman, and then earned a promotion to become managers of entire job sites or multiple ones.

However, it is becoming more common for construction managers to enter the higher echelons of the industry with advanced schooling. It is not uncommon for modern-day managers to have a two- or four-year college degree in an area such as construction science, construction management, architecture, or engineering. As technology advances, resulting in improving construction methods and techniques, building projects are becoming more complex. Advanced levels of knowledge are becoming necessary for higher-ups managing one or more road jobs.

For those who have little time (especially while working full time) to commute to classes, many two- and four-year programs can now be completed online. Middle management, laborers, and others can now concentrate on remote learning during nights and weekends.

The higher someone ascends on the construction career ladder—from laborer to foreman to superintendent or higher—the bigger the projects he or she will gain experience with.

DEGREE PROGRAMS

Students can earn two-year (associate's) degrees, often obtained at community colleges or technical schools, in construction technology or construction management. An associate's degree can be applied later toward a four-year program via credit transfer if a person chooses to continue his or her education.

In these two-year programs, students tend to concentrate on straightforward topics and skills directly needed on the job, such as surveying, elements of building, materials, construction management, cost estimating and budgeting, construction contracts, and on-site construction. In addition, the degree can often include communications classes, including coursework in public speaking and writing.

Four-year degree programs are often offered at colleges and universities. These programs can lead to a bachelor of science or bachelor of arts degree in a major such as construction management, civil engineering, building science, or civil engineering technology. These programs combine course work in construction, physics, and building with courses in the liberal arts to provide a well-rounded education.

Course work in these programs can include topics such as construction materials, engineering graphics, computer-aided design, surveying, strength of materials, hydraulics, soil mechanics, building structures, structural behavior, architecture, construction methods, foundation engineering, water and wastewater treatment, transportation engineering, and more. Students also complete courses in business and management, mathematics, physics, English, and

Construction managers can sometimes manage a paving and road-resurfacing project that is miles long, involving numerous crew teams and foremen, such as Boston's Big Dig, a megaproject, shown here, that lasted almost two decades.

communication. In four-year programs, students may also choose an area of concentration, such as structural design, water resources, or sustainable structures.

A two- or four-year degree can help prepare an employee for advancement in the construction field, as well as for jobs designing roadways and bridges, parking lots, and airport runways. These formal programs also lead to advanced leadership positions and higher pay.

LICENSES AND CERTIFICATIONS

While not a universal requirement for paving and construction managers, there are two certifications for professionals in the field. The Construction Management Association of America offers the certified construction manager designation to construction workers who have acquired the necessary years of experience plus a passing score on a technical exam. The exam covers topics related to construction management, such as the role and responsibilities of a construction manager, common legal issues faced on the job, and other topics related to construction management.

The American Institute of Constructors offers the associate constructor and certified professional constructor designations to those who meet the requirements of each license and who pass the necessary exams. These designations add value to a manager's experience, show an aptitude for construction knowledge, and can help make a candidate more attractive when searching for a management-level construction job.

CHAPTER SIX

PAVING THE WAY FOR THE FUTURE

The infrastructure field provides exciting opportunities for those with a high school diploma who enjoy building and constructing things to find rewarding jobs with good pay and opportunities for promotion. As our nation begins to focus on efforts to improve and repair infrastructure systems around the country, many jobs will need to be filled.

ADVANCED CAREERS IN ROADWORK

While there are a wide range of jobs in paving and road resurfacing that do not require formal education beyond a high school diploma, some career paths require a degree from a four-year college. Such professions include architect, civil engineer, project manager, and other higher-level positions in local, state, and federal government agencies that deal with infrastructure on a hands-on basis. For such jobs, completion of a degree program is usually a given. Thesc positions offer competitive pay and the chance to

Advanced positions in construction require college degrees in engineering, construction management, or architecture.

ascend to leadership positions. Some of these roles center on the design and development of large-scale construction projects.

Civil engineers are responsible for conceiving, designing, and supervising a wide range of infrastructure projects and systems. These can include creating new roadways, designing buildings and airports, and constructing tunnels, dams, and bridges. A bachelor's degree in civil engineering is a requirement for entry into these positions. A civil engineering degree includes course work that covers topics such as modern structures, environmental

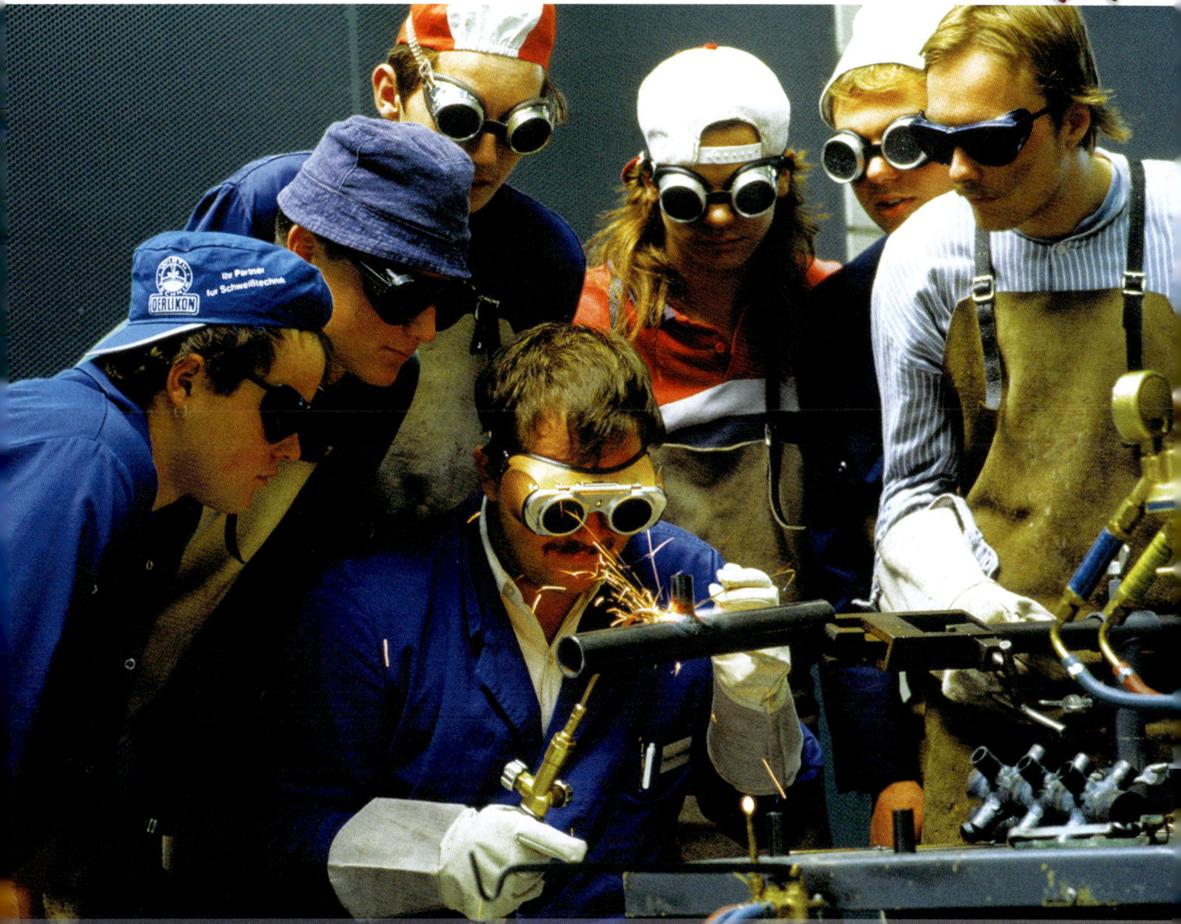

Specialized skills in welding, building design, or other areas can also be beneficial for those who want to move up to positions of leadership.

management, physics, structural dynamics, transportation engineering, mathematics, engineering systems, surveying, mechanics of solids, materials, and computer-aided design.

The job of a surveyor is a valuable one. Surveyors visit sites where work has yet to take place—for example, an existing stretch of highway or a clearing where a road is planned. There, they take exact measurements to determine property boundaries for a construction project. Those measurements become the foundation for the construction project and even mapmaking.

To become a surveyor, you'll need a two- or four-year degree in land surveying, civil engineering, or construction management. Course work covers areas such as natural resource measurement, forest ecology, remote sensing and geographic information systems, surveying computations, construction and topographic surveying, and boundary surveying.

CAREER ADVANCEMENT IN PAVING AND ROAD SURFACING

Infrastructure is a dynamic industry. It offers a wide range of career options with good pay and opportunities for advancement. To succeed and grow in the field, consider some of the following:

- **Networking.** Connect to others in your field who share the same career interests as you. These are people who can help connect you to jobs in the field, share knowledge about new developments, or educate you on what others may be doing career wise. Join an online networking website, such as LinkedIn.com, to meet people in the field and to stay on top of the latest developments.
- **Sharpening Your Skill Set.** By keeping your skills and knowledge current, you are helping yourself in your present position as well as preparing yourself for career advancement. Subscribe to blogs on infrastructure and

transportation to learn the latest news. Enroll in webinars, which are online seminars you can participate in that can offer you the most up-to-date information on skills and trends in the field.

- **Reading Up.** Leading construction companies are often awarded the biggest and best construction jobs, like building new bridges or airport runways or highway resurfacing projects. Make a list of the companies you want to work for and research their job openings. Even if you're not ready for a job right now, it's important to see what kinds of candidates they are looking for and to get a general idea of the types of qualifications these companies are looking for in a candidate.

WHAT TO DO IN HIGH SCHOOL

You can begin to prepare for a career in infrastructure, particularly road paving and resurfacing, while you're still in high school. Students should focus on completing high school level courses in mathematics (algebra, precalculus, calculus, trigonometry, and geometry) and science (biology, chemistry, physics, and earth science). These courses will help you develop the foundational skills you need to understand more complex elements of your future job, such as understanding measurements and blueprints. Taking courses in environmental science can also help you gain some knowledge of how construction projects affect the world around us.

TIPS FOR SUCCESSFUL INTERVIEWING

After applying for a job, you might be called in to interview for the position. An interview is an opportunity for you to learn more about a company, as you relate to a potential employer the skills and knowledge you can bring to the job. You can prepare for it in various ways.

First, become familiar with the company you are interviewing with by spending some time on their website. Learn who they are, what they do, and what kinds of construction or infrastructure projects they specialize in completing. If it is a large company, there may be news items about them and their work in your city, region, state, and elsewhere.

Make sure to read your résumé over. Check it for spelling and grammatical errors. While employers are more interested in your skills and suitability for a hands-on construction gig, such things can make a difference. Be prepared to talk about how your course work, previous jobs, and other experience have prepared you for the job in question.

Remember, too, that communication and being a people person are key skills in construction and other sectors. Make eye contact with your interviewer(s), be friendly, and ask questions about the job. You are an active participant in the interview, so make sure you pay attention and listen to all of what your interviewer is telling you. Don't be afraid to ask follow-up questions if you want something explained further or if you have questions about the job.

THAT FIRST JOB

Your first job is a great opportunity. Not only will you begin to earn a living, you'll also begin to learn more about the infrastructure industry and, in particular, road paving and resurfacing projects. This entry-level job is the first opportunity of many you will have during your career. While your first position will most likely be entry level, you'll be learning a lot about the industry, the basics of working on a road crew, and the skills you'll need to be successful. Look for opportunities to show initiative by taking on more responsibility. Down the line, find out if you can shadow someone in a position you'd like to hold in the future. Make sure you learn how things work in your new company, and don't be too pushy. At the same time, recognize your strengths and make sure others—namely your superiors—value and acknowledge them.

Networking with professionals, even informally via friendships, union activities, or the like, can be a great source of career advice and guidance and also job opportunities for those seeking them.

Keep a positive attitude by showing respect to veteran paving crew members and by soaking in as much knowledge as you can. Ask for feedback on your performance and for areas where you can improve. Work hard to address issues that need work, and seek out opportunities to improve where necessary.

- **What They Do:** Pavers do the manual labor involved with road construction, while surfacing-equipment operators control the machines that spread and level asphalt or spread and smooth concrete for roadways or other structures.
- **Work Environment:** Paving- and surfacing-equipment operators work in almost all types of weather conditions. Rain and extremely cold weather may be the only types of weather that can halt an outdoor construction project.
- **Work Qualifications:** A high school diploma or equivalent is required for most jobs. Vocational training and math courses are useful, and a course in auto mechanics can be helpful because workers often perform maintenance on the equipment used on the job. Course work at vocational schools may be beneficial in establishing a foundation of skills or for finding a job. Some programs may specialize in a particular brand or type of construction equipment or in the foundational knowledge of construction, construction management, or roadwork and paving.
- **Learning on the Job:** Most workers will learn the needed skills on the job, where they will begin to operate light paving and surfacing equipment under the guidance of an experienced operator. Later, as they gain skill and experience, road-paving and surfacing workers can be promoted to positions that will enable them to operate heavier equipment, such as bulldozers, rollers, and more. Some construction equipment has computerized controls. These machines may require greater skill, and more time, to learn to operate.

GLOSSARY

compensation Money paid to a worker for doing a job.

concurrently Describing two or more events happening at the same time.

dexterity Skill in performing tasks using your hands.

grade The slope of a hill or roadway.

municipal Relating to a city, town, or village's government.

pedestrian A person who walks on a roadway or sidewalk, as opposed to someone in a motor vehicle or on a bicycle.

peripheral Describing something that is happening on the edge of some place.

productivity The measure of how much work is done and how effectively and efficiently it is accomplished.

remediation The act of reversing or stopping damage occurring to the environment.

sector A distinct area within a larger one; it can specifically refer to a particular area of the larger economy, such as the construction sector.

sustainable Describing measures, processes, or technologies that help protect the environment, especially by conserving or recycling various resources.

union An organization that represents the economic interests of the workers who are represented by it.

wastewater Water that has been used in a home or business.

American Concrete Pavement Association (ACPA)
9450 W. Bryn Mawr, Suite 150
Rosemont, Illinois 60018
(847) 966-2272
Website: http://www.acpa.org
The ACPA is the world's largest trade association in the field. They represent the interests of those involved with the design, construction, and preservation of concrete pavement to state and federal government agencies and authorities that oversee roadbuilding.

American Road and Transportation Builders Association (ARTBA)
250 E Street SW, Suite 900
Washington, DC 20024
(202) 289-4434
Website: https://www.artba.org
ARTBA's goal is to protect the nation's transportation infrastructure so that our roadways can safely meet the demand of the public and of businesses for safe and efficient travel.

Asphalt Emulsion Manufacturers Association (AEMA)
800 Roosevelt Road, Building C-312
Glen Ellyn, IL 60137
(630) 942-6579
Website: http://www.aema.org
Facebook: @aema.social
Twitter: @aemahq

AEMA promotes the development and use of asphalt emulsions, which are more environmentally friendly road-paving and resurfacing materials.

Canadian Technical Asphalt Association (CTAA)
895 Fort Street, Suite 300
Victoria, BC V8W 1H7
Canada
(250) 361-9187
Email: admin@ctaa.ca
Website: https://www.ctaa.ca
Facebook: @CanadianTechnicalAsphalt
The CTAA consists of scientists, engineers, technicians, academics, students, contractors, consultants, and suppliers involved in the design, development, research, and performance of flexible pavements.

National Asphalt Paving Association (NAPA)
5100 Forbes Boulevard
Lanham, MD 20706-4407
(888) 468-6499
Website: http://www.asphaltpavement.org
Facebook: @AsphaltPavement
Twitter: @NAPATweets
The NAPA is a trade association that exclusively represents the interests of asphalt pavement material producers and paving contractors on the national level with local and national government agencies and business organizations. The group conducts research into sustainable paving materials and seeks ways to improve road-paving techniques.

National Highway Institute (NHI)
1310 North Courthouse Road, Suite 300
Arlington, VA 22201
(877) 558-6873
Website: https://www.nhi.fhwa.dot.gov
Facebook: @NationalHighwayInstitute
The NHI is known for providing up-to-date training on transportation and improvement of roadway conditions and safety of the nation's roads, highways, and bridges.

Ontario Road Builders Association (ORBA)
365 Brunel Road, Unit #1
Mississauga, ON L4Z 1Z5
Canada
(905) 507-1107
Website: http://www.ohmpa.org
Facebook: @OntarioHotMix
Twitter: @OAPC_ON_Asphalt
ORBA is the leading advocate of Ontario's transportation infrastructure industry, its contractors, and its material and service providers.

FOR FURTHER READING

Adams, Alice. *Tractor-Trailer Truck Driver Training*. Independence, KY: Delmar Cengage Learning, 2012.

Byers, Ann. *A Career as a Construction Manager* (Essential Careers). New York, NY: Rosen Publishing, 2016.

Hayes, Brian. *Infrastructure: A Guide to the Industrial Landscape*. New York, NY: W. W. Norton & Company, 2014.

Henderson, Holly, and Anthony D. Cortese. *Becoming a Green Building Professional: A Guide to Careers in Sustainable Architecture, Design, Engineering, Development, and Operations*. Hoboken, NJ: Wiley, 2012.

Leavitt, Amie Jane. *The Vo-Tech Track to Success in Architecture and Construction* (Learning a Trade, Preparing for a Career). New York, NY: Rosen Publishing Group, 2014.

Niver, Heather Moore. *Careers in Construction* (Essential Careers). New York, NY: Rosen Publishing, 2013.

Petroski, Henry. *The Road Taken: The History and Future of America's Infrastructure*. New York, NY: Bloomsbury, 2017.

Sheen, Barbara. *Careers in Architecture and Construction* (Exploring Careers). San Diego, CA: Referencepoint Press, 2016.

Speck, Jeff. *Walkable City: How Downtown Can Save America, One Step at a Time*. New York, NY: North Point Press, 2013.

Wolny, Philip. *Getting a Job in the Construction Industry* (Job Basics: Getting the Job You Need). New York, NY: Rosen Publishing, 2016.

Alpha Paving Industries, LLC. "Facts about Asphalt." Retrieved November 25, 2017. http://www.alphapavingtexas.com/faq/facts-asphalt-paving.

Ball, John. "Skills Need for HMA Paving Crew Laborer." ForConstructionPros.com. Retrieved November 25, 2017. https://www.forconstructionpros.com/asphalt/pavers/article/10117160/skills-need-for-hma-paving-crew-laborer.

Bright Network. "Key Skills You Need For: The Infrastructure Sector." Retrieved November 22, 2017. https://www.brightnetwork.co.uk/career-path-guides/energy-infrastructure/a-job-in-infrastructure/key-skills-infrastructure.

Bright Network. "What Is Involved in a Job in Infrastructure?" Retrieved November 22, 2017. https://www.brightnetwork.co.uk/career-path-guides/energy-infrastructure/a-job-in-infrastructure.

Bureau of Labor Statistics. "Construction Laborers and Helpers." Retrieved November 22, 2017. https://www.bls.gov/ooh/construction-and-extraction/construction-laborers-and-helpers.htm#tab-1.

Bureau of Labor Statistics. "Construction Managers." Retrieved November 22, 2017. https://www.bls.gov/ooh/management/construction-managers.htm#tab-1.

ConstuctionPros.com. "How to Train Your Paving Crew." Retrieved November 22, 2017. https://www.forconstructionpros.com/asphalt/article/10298667/how-to-train-your-paving-crew.

Doerer, Kristen. "The Highway Trust Fund Keeps Bridges from Falling Down, but Will Congress Reauthorize It?"

PBS NewsHour, October 27, 2015. https://www.pbs.org/newshour/economy/highway-trust-fund-keeps-bridges-falling-will-congress-pay-bill.

Hardhathub.com. "Top 3 Tips for How to Advance Your Career in the Construction Field." Retrieved November 20, 2017. https://blog.hardhathub.com/top-3-tips-advance-career-construction-industry.

Kane, Joseph, and Robert Puentes. "Beyond Shovel-Ready: The Extent and Impact of U.S. Infrastructure Jobs." Brookings Institute, May 9, 2014. https://www.brookings.edu/interactives/beyond-shovel-ready-the-extent-and-impact-of-u-s-infrastructure-jobs.

Monroe Community College/SUNY. "Construction Technology." Retrieved November 22, 2017. http://www.monroecc.edu/academics/majors-programs/stem/construction-technology-associate-degree.

New York City Department of Transportation. "Street and Roadway Construction." Retrieved November 20, 2017. http://www.nyc.gov/html/dot/html/infrastructure/construction.shtml.

Noguchi, Yuki. "Agreeing on More Money for Roads, Bridges May Be Easier Than Finding Workers." *All Things Considered*, October 28, 2016. https://www.npr.org/2016/10/28/499623017/agreeing-on-more-money-for-roads-bridges-may-be-easier-than-finding-workers.

Patterson, Thom. "How Houston's Layout May Have Made Its Flooding Worse." CNN, August 31, 2017. http://www.cnn.com/2017/08/31/us/houston-harvey-flooding-urban-planning/index.html.

Rochester Institute of Technology. "Civil Engineering Technology, BS Degree." Retrieved November 22, 2017. https://www.rit.edu/programs/civil-engineering-technology-bs.

Thomas, Lauren, and John W. Schoen. "Engineers Give America's Infrastructure a Near Failing Grade." CNBC, March 9, 2017. https://www.cnbc.com/2017/03/09/engineers-give-americas-infrastructure-a-near-failing-grade.html.

Woolner, David. "The WPA that Built America Is Needed Once Again." Roosevelt Institute, May 5, 2011. http://rooseveltinstitute.org/wpa-built-america-needed-once-again.

INDEX

ABOUT THE AUTHOR

Laura La Bella is the author of numerous nonfiction children's books. She has written several books on career fields, including *What Degree Do I Need to Pursue a Career in Bookkeeping and Accounting?*, *Internship & Volunteer Opportunities for People Who Love to Build Things* (A Foot in the Door), and *Careers in Computer Technology: Web Development*. La Bella lives in Rochester, New York, with her husband and two sons.

PHOTO CREDITS

Cover, p. 3 TFoxFoto/Shutterstock.com; pp. 6–7 © iStockphoto .com/fotoember; p. 11 SvedOliver/Shutterstock.com; p. 15 © iStockphoto.com/trekandshoot; p. 17 © iStockphoto.com/SteveDF; p. 21 © iStockphoto.com/FatCamera; p. 25 © iStockphoto.com/ KatarzynaBialasiewicz; p. 28 © iStockphoto.com/kzenon; p. 29 © iStockphoto.com/Wicki58; p. 31 Scalatore1959/iStock/Thinkstock; p. 34 Sergei Primakov/Shutterstock.com; p. 37 © iStockphoto .com/Eyjafjallajokull; p. 38 Stockr/Shutterstock.com; p. 41 Suliman Razvan/Shutterstock.com; p. 43 SeventyFour/Shutterstock.com; p. 46 WendellandCarolyn/iStock/Thinkstock; p. 48 © iStockphoto.com /Bjdlzx; p. 51 Perutskyi Petro/Shutterstock.com; p. 53 Norman Pogson/Shutterstock.com; p. 57 © iStockphoto.com/MartinLisner; p. 59 Boston Globe/Getty Images; p. 62 Phovoir/Shutterstock.com; p. 63 Maximilian Stock Ltd./The Image Bank/Getty Images; p. 68 Joe Raedle/Getty Images; interior pages background (asphalt) Thawornurak/Shutterstock.com.

Design: Nelson Sá; Layout: Nicole Russo-Duca; Editor: Philip Wolny; Photo Researcher: Sherri Jackson